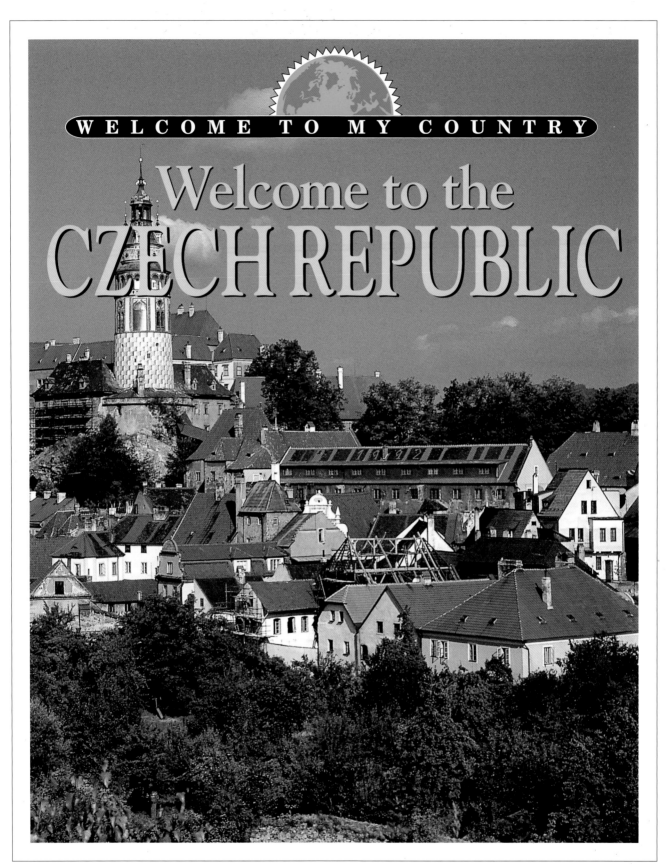

WELCOME TO MY COUNTRY

Welcome to the
CZECH REPUBLIC

Gareth Stevens Publishing
A WORLD ALMANAC EDUCATION GROUP COMPANY

Written by
GRACE PUNDYK

Edited by
MELVIN NEO

Edited in USA by
JENETTE DONOVAN GUNTLY

Designed by
GEOSLYN LIM

Picture research by
SUSAN JANE MANUEL
THOMAS KHOO

First published in North America in 2005 by
Gareth Stevens Publishing
A World Almanac Education Group Company
330 West Olive Street, Suite 100
Milwaukee, Wisconsin 53212 USA

Please visit our web site at
www.garethstevens.com
For a free color catalog describing
Gareth Stevens Publishing's list of high-quality
books and multimedia programs,
call 1-800-542-2595 (USA) or
1-800-387-3178 (Canada).
Gareth Stevens Publishing's fax: (414) 332-3567.

© **MARSHALL CAVENDISH INTERNATIONAL (ASIA)**
PRIVATE LIMITED 2005
Originated and designed by
Times Editions Marshall Cavendish
An imprint of Marshall Cavendish International (Asia) Pte Ltd
A member of Times Publishing Limited
Times Centre, 1 New Industrial Road
Singapore 536196
http://www.marshallcavendish.com/genref

Library of Congress Cataloging-in-Publication Data
Pundyk, Grace.
Welcome to the Czech Republic / Grace Pundyk.
p. cm. — (Welcome to my country)
Includes bibliographical references and index.
ISBN 0-8368-3127-6 (lib. bdg.)
1. Czech Republic — Juvenile literature. I. Title. II. Series.
DB2011.P86 2005
943.71—dc22   2004052567

Printed in Singapore

1 2 3 4 5 6 7 8 9 09 08 07 06 05

PICTURE CREDITS
Agence French Presse: 14, 15 (bottom),
    16, 17, 29, 36
Art Directors & TRIP Photo Library: 8, 19,
    23, 26, 28
Sylvia Cordaiy: 9 (top)
Focus Team—Italy: 1, 3 (all), 5, 22, 27, 33,
    40, 45
Getty Images/Hulton Archives: 10, 11,
    12, 13, 18, 25, 37
Guardian International Currency Corp.:
    44 (both)
Haga Library, Japan: 2, 4, 6, 7, 24, 30,
    31, 32, 38, 43
The Hutchison Picture Library: cover,
    20, 21, 35
Earl & Nazima Kowell: 41
Lonely Planet Images: 9 (bottom), 34, 39
North Wind Picture Archives: 15 (top)
Topham Picturepoint: 15 (center)

Digital Scanning by Superskill Graphics Pte Ltd

Contents

Words that appear in the glossary are printed in **boldface** type the first time they occur in the text.

4

Welcome to the Czech Republic

The Czech **Republic** is in Europe. It was founded in 1993 and is one of the world's youngest countries. In the past, the Czechs suffered under many rulers. Today, the Czechs are very proud of their free and growing nation. Let's visit the Czech Republic and its people!

Opposite: There are many man-made lakes in the Czech Republic. The lakes are used to raise fish, such as freshwater carp and trout.

Below: Prague Castle sits atop a hill in the city of Prague. It overlooks the Vltava River.

The Flag of the Czech Republic

The blue triangle on the Czech Republic's flag used to stand for Slovakia, which is now a separate country. Today, the triangle stands for **independence**. The white and red bands stand for the regions of Bohemia and Moravia.

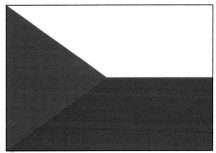

The Land

The Czech Republic is surrounded by the countries of Poland, Slovakia, Austria, and Germany. It covers about 30,400 square miles (78,740 square kilometers). The Bohemian region, in the western part of the Czech Republic, has many low mountains that surround **plateaus**, plains, and hills. Moravia, in the east, is very hilly. The country's highest point is Mount Sněžka, which stands 5,256 feet (1,602 meters) high.

Below: Much of Moravia's hilly land is used for farming.

Rivers, Lakes, and Springs

The Czech Republic has three major river systems, which are the Labe, the Odra, and the Morava. The country's longest river is the Vltava River. It is about 270 miles (435 kilometers) long. Most lakes in the Czech Republic are man made. The nation has many natural **mineral springs**. People bathe in the springs, which are said to be good for their health. Hot springs, such as those in Karlovy Vary, are popular as well.

Above:
Many bridges cut across the Vltava River. The Charles Bridge (*second bridge from the front*) is the most famous bridge. It is lined with many statues of famous people from the country's history.

Climate

In the Czech Republic's inland regions, the climate is mostly mild. Summers are warm and winters are cold. In the mountains, however, the winters are harsh. The southern Bohemian region has hot summers and mild winters. The country's average summer temperature is 68° Fahrenheit (20° Celsius). Winter temperatures average 23° F (-5° C). The country gets rain all year, but the lower areas get less rain than the mountains.

Above: A Czech boy plays in the colorful autumn leaves. The Czech Republic has four seasons.

Plants and Animals

Many kinds of plants grow in the Czech Republic. In high mountain forests, oak, spruce, and beech trees grow. In higher mountain areas, grass and lichen grow. Ash and maple trees grow in valleys.

Above: Chamois are a type of antelope. Small groups of chamois live in the mountain regions of the Czech Republic. They are known for their ability to jump from rock to rock without falling.

Many animals live in the country. In the mountain regions, animals such as wolves, brown bears, foxes, and mink are common. In the lower regions, hares and badgers are common. The country has many kinds of birds, including wild geese, ducks, eagles, vultures, and owls.

Left: Small animals called martens live in the mountains of the Czech Republic. Their fur is soft and thick. Martens only eat meat.

History

The Celtic people were the first people known to live in what is now the Czech Republic. In about the 400s A.D., Slavic tribes settled in Silesia, Bohemia, and Moravia. By the 800s, the Slavic tribes had joined to form the Great Moravian **Empire**. The Přemysl **dynasty** came to power in the 900s. They ruled Bohemia and Moravia until 1306.

Left:
Charles University was named after King Charles IV. It was founded in 1348 in the city of Prague. After the king made Prague the capital of his kingdom, the city became a center for learning.

Left: In 1618, angry Czech Protestants threw two Catholic officials out of a window of Prague Castle. The event helped lead to the Thirty Years' War. By the end of the war, Czech culture had been crushed, and the Catholic Hapsburgs ruled the whole country.

From Charles IV to the Hapsburgs

In the 1300s, the region grew under the rule of King Charles IV. In the 1400s, the Hussites, who were **reformers** from Bohemia, tried to break away from the Catholic Church. They were a threat to the power German Catholics held over Europe. In 1526, the Catholic Hapsburg dynasty took control, and Ferdinand I became king. The Hapsburgs fought the Czech people for control. The Catholics fought the Hussites and **Protestants** as well. In 1620, the Czechs were beaten. Most Czechs later became Catholic, and Czech rulers were taken out of power.

Czechoslovakia

In 1918, after World War I, the Czech lands and Slovakia joined to become Czechoslovakia. Industries, trade, the arts, and literature grew in the republic. In 1939, German Nazi troops took over. Czechoslovakians who were against the Nazis, including Czech Jews, were put in **concentration camps**, where many of them died. In 1945, Nazi rule ended when the **Allies** defeated Germany.

Below: Nazi leader Adolf Hitler stands in a passing car. He is being saluted by Sudeten Germans, a small group of Germans who lived in Czechoslovakia. Most people in the nation were against the Nazis.

Left: Angry Czechs climb onto a broken Soviet tank in the city of Prague. The Soviets took over the nation in 1968 after new freedoms were given to the Czech people. The Soviets wanted to be sure the country stayed communist.

From Communism to Democracy

After Nazi rule ended, the country's government was put back in place. In 1948, the country became **communist**. In 1968, the Soviet Union, a communist country, took over. Under harsh Soviet rule, the economy failed, and suffering became a part of everyday life for many Czechoslovakians. In 1989, the Velvet **Revolution** ended Soviet control with no violence. One of the leaders of the revolution, Václav Havel, became the first president to be elected after the country became a **democracy** again.

The Birth of the Czech Republic

On January 1, 1993, Czechoslovakia became two countries, Slovakia and the Czech Republic. The separation was called the "Velvet Divorce." Because Václav Havel had a hard time accepting the split, he stepped down as president. Later in 1993, he was elected president of the Czech Republic. The nation now belongs to important groups, such as the North Atlantic Treaty Organization (NATO). In 2004, the country joined the European Union.

Left: In February 2003, President Václav Havel (*right*) left office. Václav Klaus (*left*) was elected the new president of the Czech Republic.

Jan Hus (c. 1369–1415)

In 1396, Jan Hus became a priest. He wrote *De Ecclesiâ*, which said negative things about the Catholic Church. In 1415, he was burned at the stake. The Hussites named themselves after him.

Maria Theresa

Maria Theresa (1717–1780)

In 1740, Maria Theresa became the empress of the Hapsburg lands. She opposed the power that the Catholic **nobles** held. She made changes to help improve the lives of the people.

František Palacký (1798–1876)

František Palacký wrote the *History of the Czech People*. It changed the way later leaders thought. He is called the father of the modern Czech nation.

František Palacký

Alexander Dubček (1921–1992)

In 1968, Alexander Dubček gave the Czech people more freedoms, but the Soviets took control. He was forced to leave. He returned in 1989 and became chairman of the Federal Assembly.

Alexander Dubček

Government and the Economy

The Czech Republic's government has three branches. The president chooses a prime minister and a cabinet, or group of advisors. Together, they make up the executive branch, which creates rules for the government and also runs it. The legislative, or lawmaking, branch is a parliament with two parts, a Senate and a Chamber of Deputies. The judicial branch runs the courts. It has a Supreme Court and a **Constitutional** Court.

Left: Czech prime minister Vladimír Špidla (*far left*) listens as Vojtěch Filip (*far right*), a Communist deputy, speaks. The men are at a meeting of parliament to discuss sending Czech soldiers to Iraq.

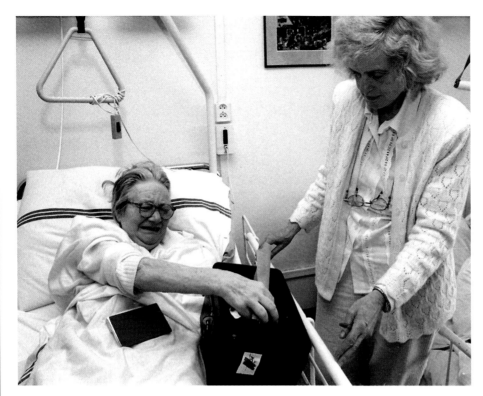

Left: In the Czech Republic, all people over age eighteen can vote. This 81-year-old woman casts her vote from her hospital bed during the general elections of 1998.

When the Czech Republic became a separate country on January 1, 1993, it adopted a new constitution. It includes rules for respecting human rights. It also states that the Czech people have the power in the nation. Through their votes, they help decide how the three branches of government are run.

The country is divided into thirteen regions, which are called *kraje* (KRA-ay). Prague, the capital city, is its own region. The nation's main government offices are located in Prague Castle.

Left: Coal supplies more than half of the energy in the Czech Republic, but it has caused a lot of pollution. To help save the land from even more damage, some nuclear power plants, including the Temelín plant (*left*), were built.

The Economy

The economy of the Czech Republic is growing. The country has highly skilled workers and good public services. The nation has grown faster than almost any other nation that used to be communist.

Before joining the European Union in 2004, the Czech Republic worked to meet the union's rules and to increase trade with other countries in the union. In turn, the European Union has given money to the Czech Republic to help the economy grow and to improve the country's public services even more.

More than half of all Czechs work in service industries, including health care and tourism. Many people also work in manufacturing. The Czechs are famous for making glass and crystal. They also make items such as automobiles, iron, steel, chemicals, and cloth.

A small number of Czechs work in farming. They grow crops such as corn, potatoes, wheat, barley, and rye. Many farmers also raise animals, including cattle, hogs, poultry, and sheep. Many of these products are **exported**.

Left: These men are assembling a car for the Škoda Company, which employs more than 24,000 workers in the Czech Republic. The automobile industry is growing in the country.

People and Lifestyle

Most people in the Czech Republic are Bohemian. Some people are Moravian or Slovak. Small groups of people in the country are German, Roma, Polish, Silesian, or Vietnamese.

Under communist rule, the Czech Republic had no **social classes**. Today, most Czechs still feel that their status in society should come from their own knowledge, abilities, and education. Most Czechs have a strong sense of pride in their country.

Below: Czech men and women dance in a park. The lives of Czechs are now getting longer. The Czechs born today will live about five years longer than the Czechs born during the 1970s.

Czech Roma

Between 150,000 and 300,000 Roma live in the Czech Republic. In the past, the Roma were called "gypsies." Many experts believe that the Roma moved to Europe from India in the 1400s. In the Czech Republic, many Roma suffer from **discrimination**. The government has tried to improve life for the Roma, but many Czechs still treat them badly. Some Roma are victims of hate crimes.

Left:
Two young Czech children play while their grandmother watches over them. Most Czech families are small.

Family Life

Most Czechs live in apartments in large cities. Housing is very expensive and hard to find. After marriage, many adult Czechs live with their parents until they can find their own homes. In most Czech families, the *babička* (BAHB-ish-ka), or grandmother, is respected and loved. Often, she cares for her grandchildren while their parents work. Most Czech women work full time outside of the home. Many women also take care of the house and raise the children, too.

Marriage

In the past, most Czechs married young. Today, in the countryside, many Czechs still do marry young. In cities, though, most Czechs marry later. Many of them get married later because they do not have enough money to start a family.

Some Czechs have traditional village weddings. At the wedding, people often sing, dance, and eat special meals. Most brides and grooms and their guests wear traditional costumes with many patterns of fancy sewing on them.

Below: This Czech groom is sawing a piece of wood. It is a tradition during Czech weddings.

Education

Education is considered important in the Czech Republic. Almost all Czechs can read and write. Children start basic, or elementary, school at age six. They attend for nine years. Czech children study subjects such as mathematics, art, history, music, and Czech language and literature. Students earn a *Vysvědčeni* (VEES-vehd-cheh-nee) diploma when they complete elementary school.

Below: Most Czech schools are taught using the Czech language, but some schools teach in English or German.

Secondary Schools and Universities

Czech students must take an exam to enter a secondary school. They choose from three kinds of secondary schools: technical, vocational, and gymnasium. Technical and vocational schools both prepare students for professions. In a gymnasium school, students prepare for a university. The country has twenty-three universities. Charles University in Prague is the oldest university in central Europe. It is also the Czech Republic's highest-ranked university.

Religion

Under the Czech Republic's communist government, the Czechs had very few religious freedoms. When communism ended in 1989, the Czechs were able to attend church freely. Despite this new freedom, in 2002, almost half of all Czechs still said they do not believe in any religion. Most Czechs who do practice a religion are Christian. The religion came to Bohemia in the 800s.

Above: Catholic priests celebrate a Mass outdoors on a Sunday morning. Roman Catholics make up the largest religious group in the Czech Republic.

In the 900s, the land that is now the Czech Republic came under the control of the Holy Roman Empire. During that time, many Czechs became Catholic. In the 1500s, many Czechs began to join the Protestant Church. Some Czechs are still Protestant today. Before the Nazis took over in 1939, almost 360,000 Jews lived in the Czech Republic. Most of them died in the **Holocaust**. Only a few thousand Jews live in the country today. Most of them live in the city of Prague.

Below: The Jewish cemetery in Prague is a reminder of the thousands of Czech Jews who died in the Holocaust.

Language

Czech is the official language of the Czech Republic. It is called a western Slavic language. When Czech was first written, it used Slavic characters. Later, the Roman alphabet replaced the Slavic characters. In the 1400s, reformer Jan Hus created a new set of letters. Hus used marks placed over the letters of the Roman alphabet to show Czech pronunciations and sounds.

Below: A woman in Prague walks past a wall covered with posters. Most of the people in the Czech Republic read and speak in the Czech language. Other languages spoken in the nation include Slovak, Hungarian, Polish, German, and Romany, which is the Roma language.

Left: Milan Kundera (*right*) is a famous Czech-born writer. He is best known for his two books *The Unbearable Lightness of Being,* written in 1984, and *Immortality* (1990). In 1975, he moved to France with his wife (*left*).

Literature

Over time, the Czech Republic has been home to many world-famous authors and thinkers. Czech author Jan Ámos Komenský wrote about how education can improve society. He is sometimes called "the teacher of nations." In 1984, poet Jaroslav Seifert became the first Czech to be awarded the Nobel Prize in literature. Franz Kafka was one of the most important writers of the 1900s. He wrote the famous book *Metamorphosis.*

Arts

Architecture

Over time, many beautiful examples of European architecture have been built in the Czech Republic. Saint Vitus's Cathedral, a large Gothic-style church, has a ceiling built in a pointed arch. In the 1500s, the **Renaissance** style was popular in Bohemia. By the late 1800s, the flowery ironwork of the Czech Art Nouveau style was a favorite. Today, in Prague, modern styles are popular.

Left: This building in Prague's Old Town Square was built in the Baroque style, which was popular during the late 1600s. This style features many fancy carvings and some frescoes, or pictures painted as part of the walls.

Left: The National Theater is a symbol of great pride for Czechs. The first performance at the theater was Bedřich Smetana's *Libuše*. It was an opera that told the story of the founding of Prague.

Czech Theater and Films

Czech theater has been an important voice for the Czech people since the twelfth century. Under Nazi and Communist rule, Czech theater was **censored**. Even so, during the 1950s, Czech stage design, ballet, mime, and puppet theater became very popular.

In the late twentieth century, Czech moviemakers gained attention. Czech-born director Miloš Forman won Oscar awards for his films *One Flew Over the Cuckoo's Nest* and *Amadeus*. Today, Czech filmmakers create more than a thousand films and cartoons each year.

Music

Music has been an important part of Czech life since the ninth century. In the eleventh century, Czech music consisted mostly of Gregorian **chants** and religious songs. In 1787, famous Austrian composer Wolfgang Amadeus Mozart first conducted his opera *Don Giovanni* at Prague's Nostitz Theater. Most of the nation's opera houses were built during the 1700s. Czech composer Bedřich Smetana wrote *My Country*. It is played at the opening of each Prague Spring International Music Festival.

Czech folk music dates back to the 1400s. In the 1800s, the polka, a lively form of folk dance music, was created in Bohemia. Many Czechs still enjoy folk music at festivals and celebrations.

In the 1920s, jazz became popular in the country. The Nazis and Communists tried to control jazz because it was seen as a way to **protest**. Today, many styles of jazz are popular, including big band, swing, and fusion. Other music styles, such as rock and pop, are also popular.

Below:
Street musicians often can be seen performing on the streets of Prague. They play many styles of music, including classical, folk, and jazz.

Leisure

Many Czechs belong to *Sokol* (SOH-kohl), which means falcon in Czech. It is a physical education club. Sokol was founded in 1862 by Miroslav Tyrš. He believed that sports help raise the level of national pride and health in Czech citizens. Sokol is now an important part of Czech culture. The club has 180,000 members and supports fifty-seven types of sports. Other nations now have Sokol clubs, too, including the United States.

Below:
Many Czechs enjoy playing ice hockey or skating on the frozen Vltava River during the winter.

Enjoying the Outdoors

In the winter, Czechs enjoy outdoor ice-skating on the country's frozen ponds and rivers. Downhill skiing, **tobogganing**, cross-country skiing, and snowboarding are also popular winter activities. In the warmer months, many Czechs enjoy fishing, canoeing, and swimming. The country's national parks and mountains attract mountain bikers, hikers, and rock climbers. In the Moravian Karst region, many people go caving. Czechs and foreign tourists both enjoy visiting spa resorts and springs.

Above: In summer, many Czechs enjoy spending time at a *chata* (KHAH-tah), or **chalet** in the countryside. These retired people are sharing a meal and playing cards in front of their chata.

Sports

Soccer is the most popular sport in the Czech Republic. Many children attend soccer training camps during the year. Ice hockey is also a popular sport. In 1998, the national hockey team won an Olympic gold medal. The team also has won ten World Hockey Championships. Czechs also enjoy volleyball and golf.

Many world-famous athletes come from the Czech Republic. Runner Emil Zátopek has set eighteen world records in track and field. He also has won four Olympic gold medals.

Left: Jan Železný is a Czech athlete. He is throwing a long metal spear, called a javelin, as far as he can. Železný is the only three-time gold medal winner for javelin throwing in Olympic history.

Many Czech athletes have won medals in the Olympics. Gymnast Věra Čáslavská won several Olympic medals in 1964 and 1968. Štěpánka Hilgertová won a gold medal for women's slalom canoeing in 2000. Aleš Valenta won an Olympic gold medal for freestyle skiing in 2002. He also set a world record.

Tennis is becoming very popular in the country, mainly because of famous Czech tennis players such as Ivan Lendl and Martina Navrátilová. Many young tennis players now go to tennis camps and learn from professional coaches.

Left:
This boy is swatting a woman with his *pomlázka* (PO-mlah-skah). It is a bunch of braided willow branches. When a boy swats a woman with his pomlázka, it is said to bring good health and youth to the woman.

Holidays

The Czech people celebrate holidays all through the year. During the communist years, festivals that began as religious holidays were made nonreligious. Since 1989, many Czech people have begun to celebrate them as religious holidays again. Easter is a joyful holiday for the Czechs. In the week before Easter, boys run through the streets making loud noises with wooden rattles. Girls make *kraslice* (KRAH-slih-zee), or fancy decorated eggs, on Easter Sunday.

Christmas

Before Christmas, many Czech families pick branches from cherry trees. The branches are kept in a warm place until they bloom. December 6 is Mikuláš, or Saint Nicholas Day. On Mikuláš eve, children hope that Saint Nicholas will come. If they are good, they may get small gifts and candy. If they are bad, they may receive potatoes, coal, or a rock. On Christmas Eve, families often gather for a traditional meal. Afterward, most family members exchange gifts.

Left: This man is selling carp, which is a type of fish. It is a tradition for Czech families to eat carp and potato salad on Christmas Eve. Some families buy two carp. They eat one on Christmas Eve and release one into a river after Christmas.

Food

Food in the Czech Republic is a mix of many cooking styles, including Celtic, Slavonic, German, and Hungarian. The main meal of the day is usually lunch. Most Czechs have only coffee and rolls for breakfast. Usually, dinners are only bread, meats, and cheeses. Most Czech lunches start with soup, such as potato or liver dumpling soup. The main dish is usually meat, such as pork, beef, or fish. Often, it is served with potatoes, rice, dumplings, or *sauerkraut* (SOW-er-krowt), which is pickled cabbage.

Left: This waiter is making a dessert crepe, which is a kind of pancake. Most Czechs eat in restaurants only on special occasions. Today, many young Czechs are starting to go to restaurants more often.

Many Czechs eat dessert after their meals. Popular desserts include tarts, pancakes, and apple strudel, a kind of stuffed pastry. Dumplings are popular as well. They are eaten as a side dish or as a dessert. When dumplings are eaten for dessert, they are usually filled with fruit, such as blueberries.

Most Czechs have their drinks after a meal. Many Czech children drink fruit juices or sodas. Many adults drink *pivo* (PEE-voh), or beer. Some adults drink plum brandy, liquors made from herbs, and Moravian wines as well.

Above: This man is enjoying a beer at a *hospoda* (HO-spoh-dah), or beer hall. Many Czechs go to hospodas to meet and drink beer with their friends. Each year, the Czech people drink more beer than anyone else in the world.

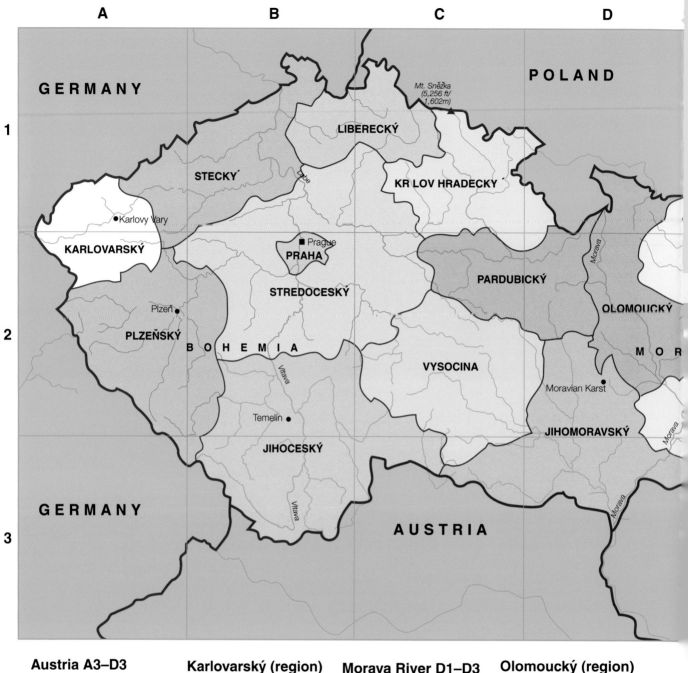

A B C D

GERMANY

POLAND

Mt. Sněžka (5,256 ft/ 1,602m)

1

LIBERECKÝ

STECKÝ

KR LOV HRADECKY

•Karlovy Vary

KARLOVARSKÝ

Prague
PRAHA

STREDOCESKÝ

PARDUBICKÝ

OLOMOUCKÝ

Plzeň•

PLZEŇSKÝ

2

B O H E M I A

Vltava

VYSOCINA

M O R

•Moravian Karst

Temelín •

JIHOCESKÝ

JIHOMORAVSKÝ

Vltava

GERMANY

3

AUSTRIA

Austria A3–D3

Bohemia A1–B3

Germany A1–C1

Jihoceský (region) B2–C3
Jihomoravský (region) C3–D3

Karlovarský (region) A1–A2

Karlovy Vary A1
Královéhradecký (region) C1–D2

Labe River B1–C2
Liberecký (region) B1–C1

Morava River D1–D3
Moravia C2–E2
Moravian Karst D2
Moravskoslezský (region) D2–E2
Mount Sněžka C1

Odra River D2–E2

Olomoucký (region) D1–E2

Pardubický (region) C2–D2
Plzeň A2
Plzeňský (region) A2–B3
Poland C1–E2
Prague B2

E

- International Boundary
- Regional Boundary
- ■ Capital
- ● City
- ▲ Highest Point
- River

Silesia

Odra

MORAVSKOSLEZSKÝ

AVIA

ZLÍNSKÝ

N

SLOVAKIA

Above: Tourists rest below a statue on Charles Bridge in Prague.

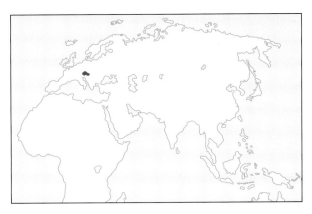

Praha (Prague region) B2

Silesia D2–E2
Slovakia D3–E3
Stredoceský (region) A2–C2

Temelín B2

Ústecký (region) A1–B1

Vltava River B1–B3
Vysocina (region) C2–D2

Zlínský (region) D2–E3

Quick Facts

Official Name   Czech Republic (Ceská Republika)

Capital   Prague (Praha)

Official Language   Czech

Population   10,246,178 (July 2004 estimate)

Land Area   30,400 square miles (78,740 square km)

Regions   13 regions (kraje) and one capital city: Jihoceský, Jihomoravský, Karlovarský, Královéhradecký, Liberecký, Moravskoslezský, Olomoucký, Pardubický, Plzeňský, Stredocesky, Ústecký, Vysocina, Zlínský, and Prague (Praha).

Highest Point   Mount Sněžka at 5,256 feet (1,602 m)

Major Rivers   Vltava River, Labe River, Odra River, and the Morava River

Religions   no religion (39.8 percent), Roman Catholics (39.2 percent), Protestant (4.6 percent), Orthodox (3 percent), other (13.4 percent)

Holidays   Easter Sunday (between March 22 and April 25), Czech Founding Day (October 28), Christmas (December 24-26)

Currency   Euro (Euro 0.92 = U.S. $1 as of May 2004)

Opposite: The capital city of Prague is home to the Valdstejn Palace.

Glossary

Allies: a group of countries during World War II that worked together to fight Germany, Italy, and Japan.

censored: reviewed to see if anything goes against a group's laws and ideas.

chalet: a cottage with exposed beams.

chants: sounds or words that are sung or repeated over and over again.

communist: regarding a government that owns and controls all property.

concentration camps: camps where people are kept prisoner.

constitutional: regarding a nation's set of laws, including citizen rights.

democracy: a government in which the citizens elect their leaders by vote.

discrimination: the practice of treating some people better than others.

dynasty: a series of rulers who rule over a long time and are from one family.

empire: a very large collection of lands or regions ruled by one group.

exported: sold and shipped from one country to another country.

Holocaust: the killing of many Jews and other Europeans by the Nazis during World War II.

independence: the state of being free from control by others.

mineral springs: springs that are soaked with chemicals from the ground.

nobles: members of the upper class who usually come from royal families.

plateaus: wide, flat areas of land that are surrounded by lower land.

protest (v): to argue strongly against someone or something.

Protestants: a group of Christians who broke away from the Catholic religion in the 1500s.

reformers: people who try to improve a situation by fixing problems they see.

Renaissance: a style using features from old Greek or Roman art and buildings.

republic: a country in which citizens elect their own lawmakers.

revolution: a sudden or total exchange of one government for another.

social classes: ranks given to people in society, often based on being part of high-ranking or low-ranking families.

tobogganing: riding long, narrow sleds.

traditional: regarding customs or styles passed down through the generations.

More Books to Read

Children of Slovakia. World's Children series. Sheila Kinkade (Carolrhoda Books)

Christmas in Prague. Bookworm series. Joyce Hannam (Oxford)

Czech Republic. Changing Faces of series. Jacob Rihosek (Raintree)

Czech Republic. Country Insights series. Rob Humphreys (Raintree)

Czech Republic. Festivals of the World series. Tim Nollen (Gareth Stevens)

Czech Republic in Pictures. Visual Geography series. Stacy Taus-Bolstad (Lerner Publishing Group)

Eva's Summer Vacation: A Story of the Czech Republic. Jan Machalek (Soundprints)

I Never Saw Another Butterfly: Children's Drawings and Poems from Terezin Concentration Camp 1942-1944. Hana Volavkova, editor (Schocken)

The Three Golden Keys. Peter Sis (Farrar, Straus, and Giroux)

Videos

Globe Trekker: Czech Republic and Southern Poland (555 Productions)

National Geographic Traveler: Prague & the Czech Republic (Questar)

Eastern Cities: Prague, Budapest and Istanbul. Travel the World series. (Questar)

Web Sites

www.infoplease.com/ipa/ A0107456.html

www.myczechrepublic.com

www.mzv.cz/washington

www.pis.cz/a/index.html

Due to the dynamic nature of the Internet, some web sites stay current longer than others. To find additional web sites, use a reliable search engine with one or more of the following keywords to help you locate information about the Czech Republic. Keywords: *Bohemian Kingdom, Czechoslovakia, Havel, Prague,* and *Velvet Revolution.*

Index